Jane Kats

MOUSEMATICS

Learning Math the Fun Way

Workbook of Logic Problems
for children ages 5–6

Dear parents and teachers!

You now have in your hands a far from ordinary workbook for the ordinary subject of mathematics.

There is a multitude of books and aids that help preschoolers become familiar with mathematics. All these aids introduce children to the world of numbers and geometric figures, teach them to tell numbers apart, continue patterns, and find identical pictures. The problems and tasks presented in all these books are more or less similar: connect identical shapes, find the odd one out in a set, count the number of objects, add or subtract, find the largest object, connect the dots to write the number 3, number 4, number 5, and so on.

However, the standard exercises conceal several dangers. First, they perpetuate unnecessary stereotypes to which the child quickly becomes accustomed. For instance, if the child needs to find an odd one out in a set, there may be only one correct answer. If the child is asked to match identical figures, there will be exactly one match for each figure, and the counterpart will be located in a different column. The child perceives the instructions and solutions as the "rules of the game" and learns to follow them, and is stumped by the smallest exception to these rules – say, there are two different ways to exclude an extra object or there are three matching shapes. There are also hidden, but pervasive visual stereotypes: children often memorize images and connect them with the required words; for instance, they know that a picture with dots drawn in the corners of a square is called "four", and an identical picture with an extra dot in the middle is called "five". But can they recognize the same number five if it looks different?

These stereotypes interfere with a child's ability to master counting, and constrict the child's freedom of thought. Therefore, in this workbook we try to break as many stereotypes as possible.

• In some problems, we have two correct solutions (a pair of friends can split a chocolate bar in different ways); some problems lack an answer (an odd number of objects cannot be divided in two). After all, in mathematics no solution is also a solution.

• A matching pair of shapes can be found in the same column.

• We build geometric figures using not only the usual squares, but also diamonds, trapezoids, and triangles:

• When the child is asked to find a number value, we use a variety of shapes in addition to dots: diamonds, crosses, anything. Also, their arrangements in the boxes are random, unlike the standard dice configurations.

Second, often the same types of exercises do not change throughout the book, so children become used to them and complete them robotically. On the one hand, this is good: children master certain operations and gain useful skills. On the other hand, if they are subsequently asked to quickly switch to a similar problem but with a larger number range (1 to 10), they might have not had enough time to really master counting to five, so they will start trying to guess the correct answer. Their guesses will be based on what they learned from previous exercises, or on the look in the teacher's eyes; or they will just try shooting in the dark. In order to avoid robotic guessing, we take the following measures:

• Quantity, numbers, digits, and their relationships to each other are approached from several angles, including unorthodox ones;

• Exercises of the same type become gradually more complicated;

• All tasks stay within the 1 to 5 counting range, so that the child has ample time to understand the concepts introduced and master counting these numbers.

Third, always doing the same exercises is just boring. Yet, mathematics includes so many beautiful and interesting topics! We have tried to create this workbooks as a compilation of unconventional, not obvious tasks that are easily understandable for five- and six-year-olds. While doing so, we have focused not on counting itself, for its own sake, but on the fact that it might be interesting to think and find your own solutions. Therefore, in this workbook:

• We alternate problems of different type.

• Most of the problems have elements of games and metaphors that children can relate to, including "Number Snakes" and "Hungry Crocodiles" (to easily explain the use of 'greater than' sign to children); bunnies and kittens hiding behind fences; entryways and floors of tall apartment buildings; as well as many other fun, child-friendly, engaging details.

• There are even entirely new types of tasks, created in our Moscow-based children's math club called "Fun Mathematics". These include exercises with counting sticks (to make geometric shapes), problems about birds in cages, games with size pointers ("I'm bigger than you!"), and puzzles about brothers and sisters.

Additionally, it is important for children to know that mathematics is not just a set of disconnected formulas that need to be memorized. We use mathematics all the time: looking for the right number in an elevator, finding the right train car, splitting a chocolate bar, counting change in a store (to see if we have enough to buy ice cream with). Math workbooks for children need to have games and objects from daily life and the child's home: building blocks, cars, trains, beads, apple halves, etc. Then, the child will be able to associate them with his or her own life experiences. It is important to show children that mathematics is not a detached subject, but a part of daily life.

Quite possibly, some exercises will seem overly difficult to children. In that case, you can try playing similar games with counting sticks, building blocks, or Lego bricks. For instance, consider a memory problem that asks which sticks were moved in a pattern. If it was too hard to solve the workbook problem with drawn sticks, it will likely be easy to do with actual sticks or toothpicks laid out on the table! Ask the child to arrange five counting sticks in the same pattern, then move one of the sticks and ask which one was moved. Then switch roles – have the child ask you a question, set a problem for you. It is also important for the child to see you engaged. More ideas for mathematical games with young children can be found in my book Math for Dessert.

Naturally, a game with real objects is more interesting and effective than a written exercise. Still, after playing counting sticks with dad, or beading some necklaces with mom, the child will easily and happily solve similar problems in this workbook.

We hope that using this workbook will be interesting and fun for both children and their caregivers!

 Harder Exercises

 Exercises with multiple solutions

 Exercises for children who can read

Match

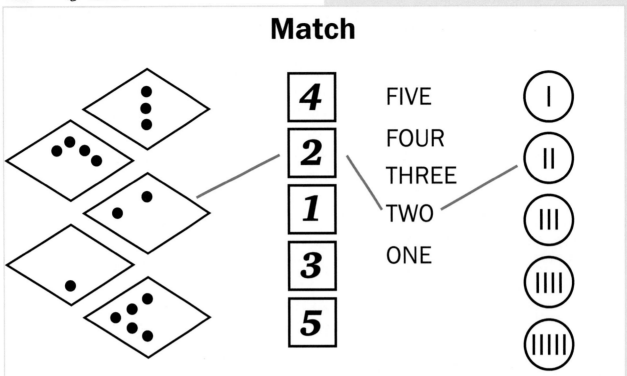

Connect the same

SHAPES COLORS

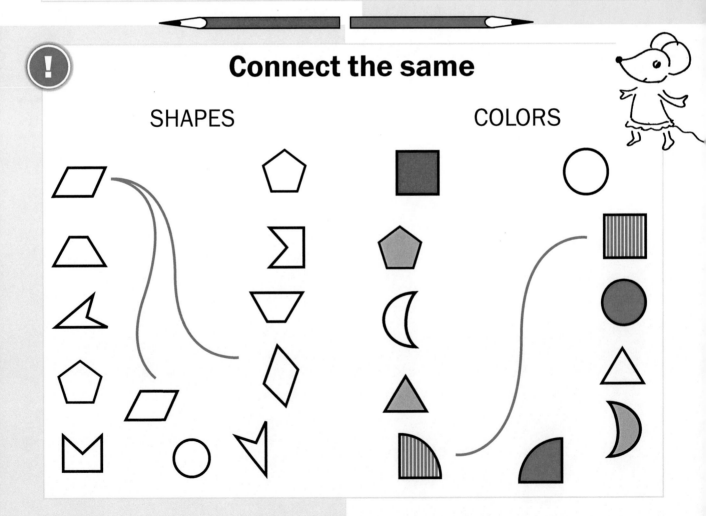

Circle the pictures made with 5 sticks

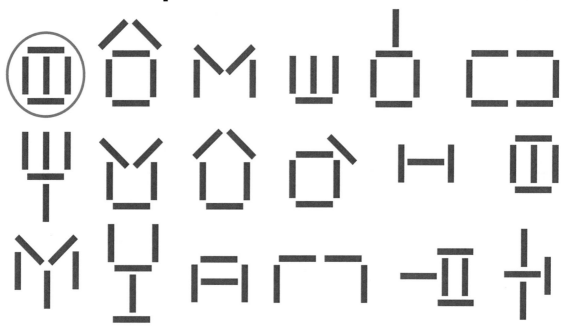

Divide the figures into domino shapes. How many are there?

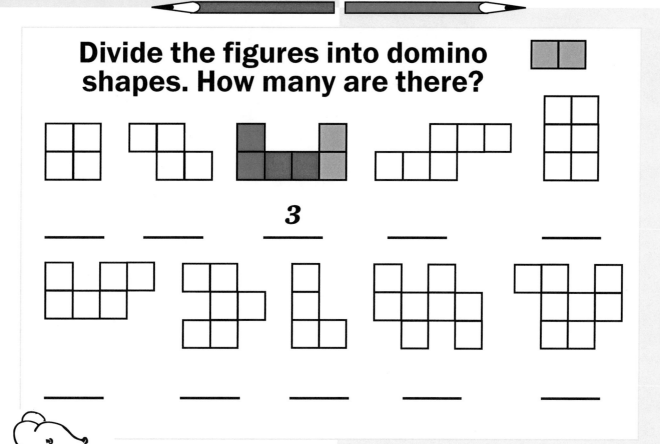

3

How many bunnies are hiding behind the fence?

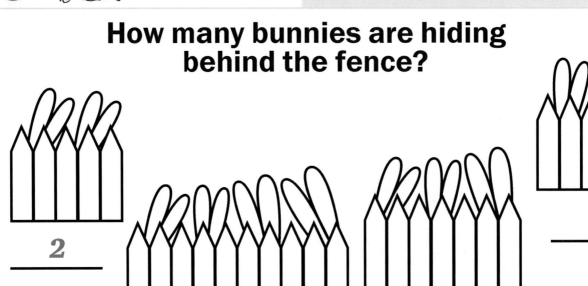

2 _____

_____

_____

_____

Use red to color the windows in the second train car

Use blue to color the second to last train car

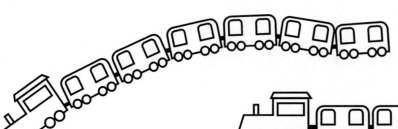

Color the engines that are pulling 5 cars

Make necklaces for Mary Mouse
Like this:

Find the matching pairs of mittens

Draw a pair for the mitten that's left over

Aa Use blue to circle the words with 3 letters
Use red to circle the words with 4 letters

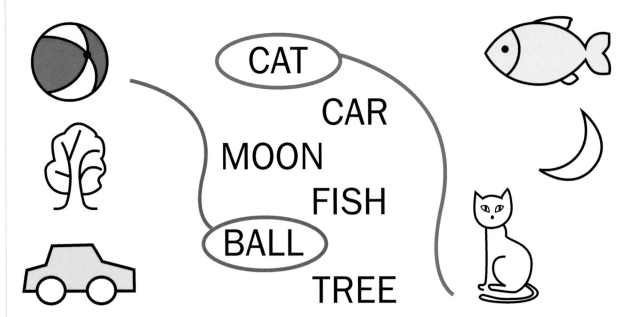

CAT

CAR

MOON

FISH

BALL

TREE

Draw in the symbols as shown

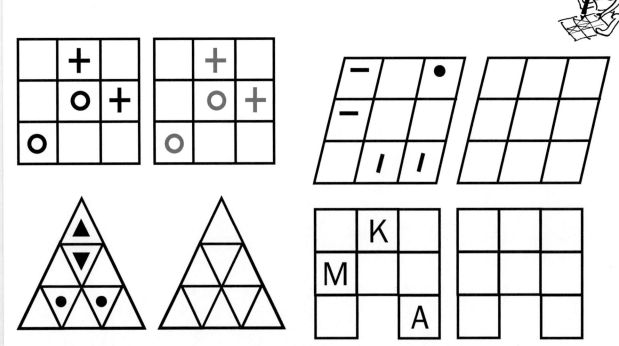

Use blue to color the shapes made of 4 squares

Use red to color the shapes made of 5 squares

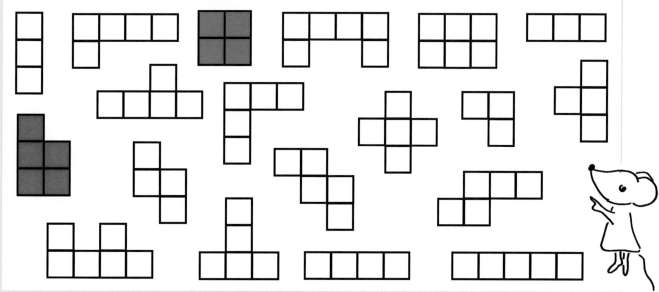

Make necklaces to look like this one:

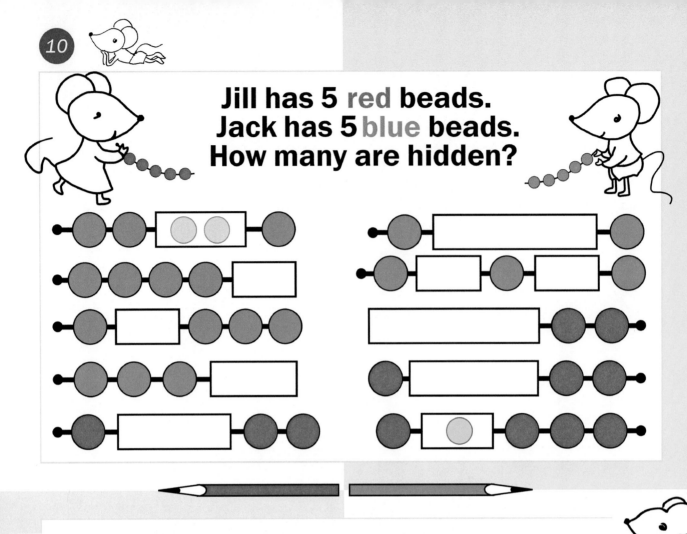

Jill has 5 red beads.
Jack has 5 blue beads.
How many are hidden?

Pick 5 windows in each house
and color them in different ways

Use blue to color the figures made of 4 shapes
Use red to color the figures made of 5 shapes

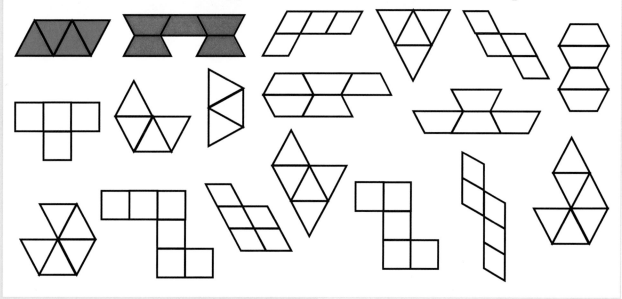

⭐ **This mouse has many nooks in her house. What does she store in each?**

L – Left   **R** – Right

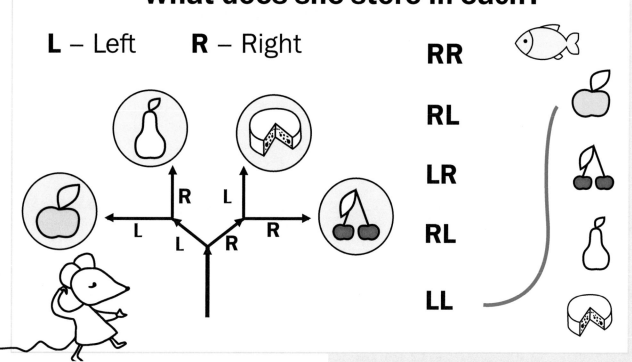

RR

RL

LR

RL

LL

★ This house has 2 entrances and 3 levels.
Who lives where?

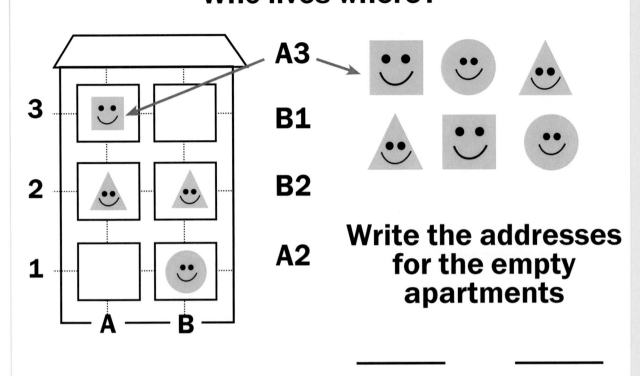

A3

B1

B2

A2

Write the addresses for the empty apartments

_____   _____

How many sticks where removed?
Replace the missing sticks

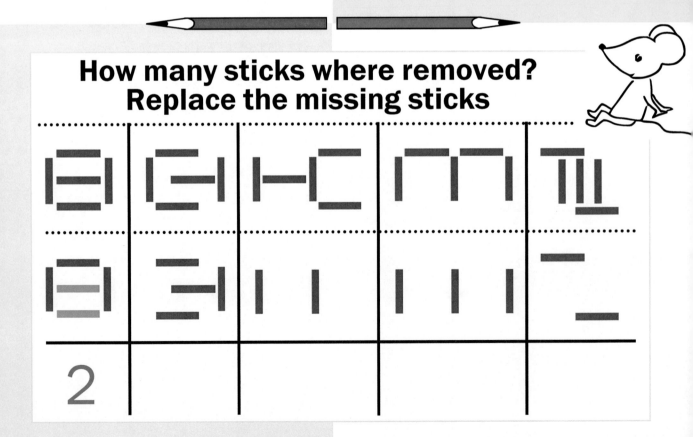

2

Help Jack and Jill split each chocolate into two equal parts

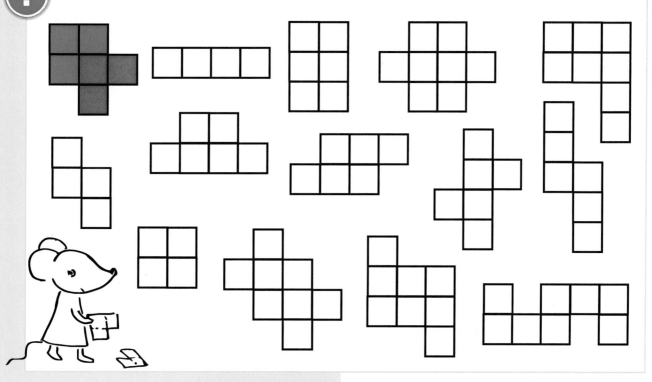

These are number worms. Write in the missing numbers. Color the heads and tails red

Use blue to color the cards with 4 dots
Use red to color the cards with 5 dots

Fill in the blanks in the charts

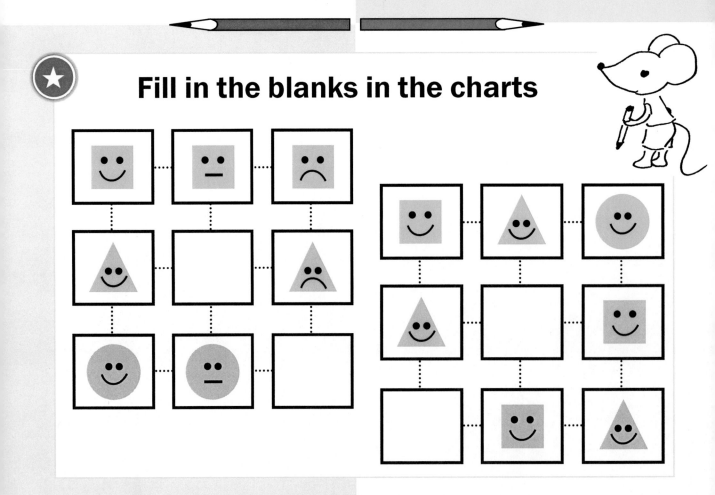

Make the pairs match

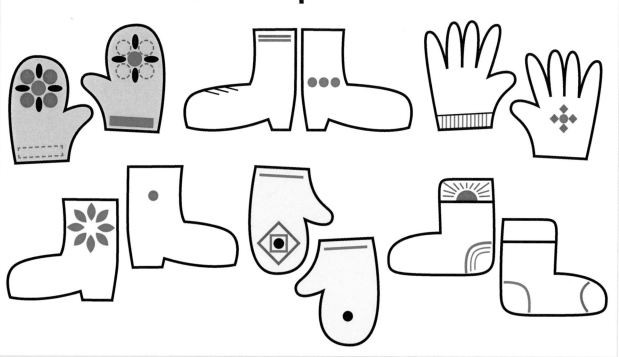

Connect dots to numbers

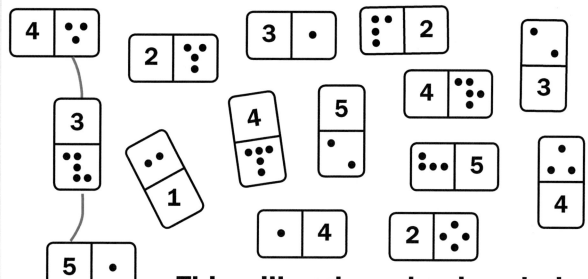

This will make a domino chain

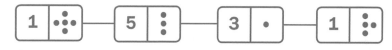

Put in the arrows

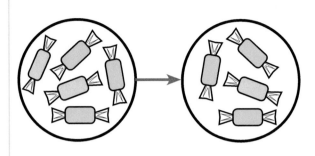

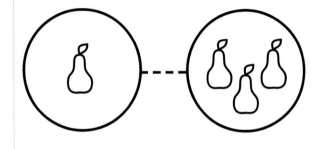

I'm greater than you!

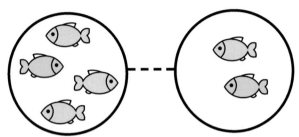

Find this number snake:

4	2	**3**
5	**1**	**2**

6	3	4
1	2	5

1	3	4
5	2	1

1	1	4
2	3	2

2	1	3	1
3	5	4	5

1	1	5	4
3	2	3	1

5	2	3	2
3	1	1	4

1	4	3	2	1

1	4	1	2	3

Where will the bird stop? Color the end square

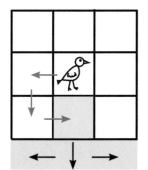 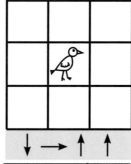 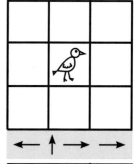

 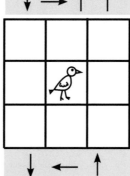 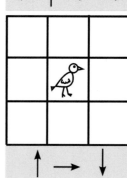

Find the garages with the same sets of cars

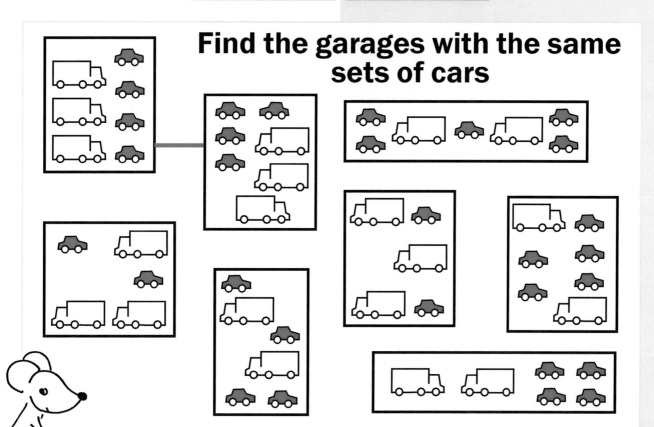

How many fingers are hidden?

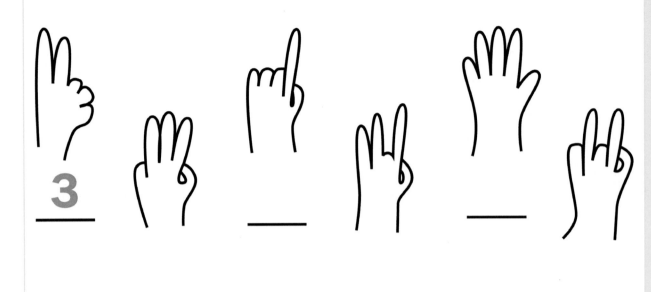

3

Make these pairs identical

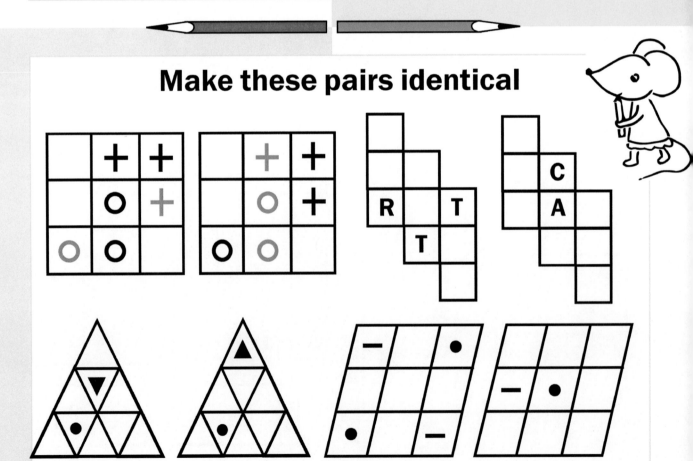

⭐ Color brothers blue, and sisters red

⊗ I don't know who this is
● girl
● boy

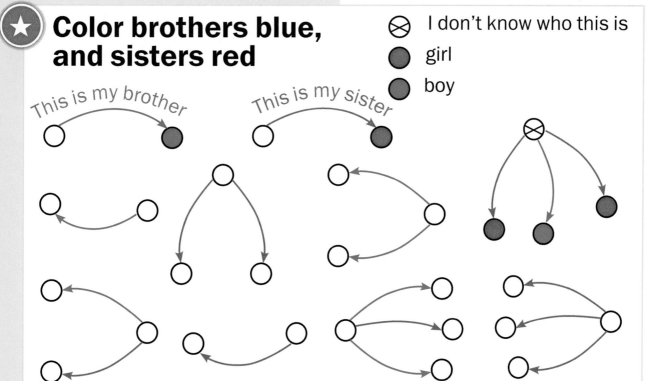

This is my brother

This is my sister

Make necklaces with a total of 5 dots. Draw in the missing dots

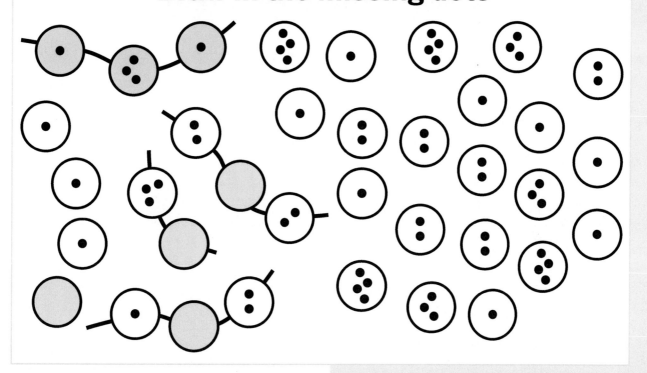

How many chickens are behind the fence?

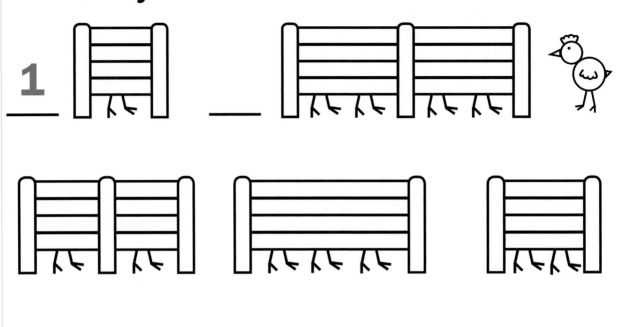

Find the towers made from the same sets of blocks. Color them the same

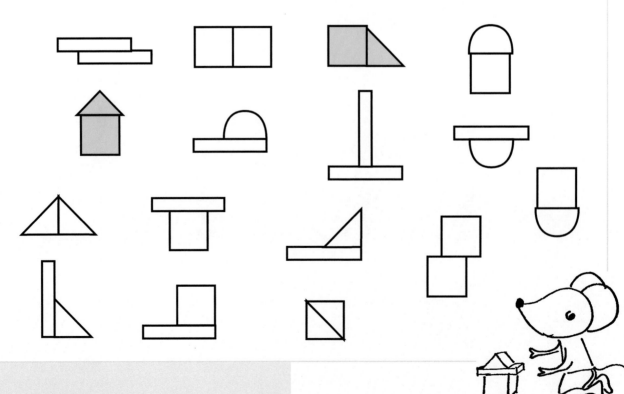

Help Jack and Jill split each chocolate into two equal parts

These are number worms. Write in the missing numbers

Circle the groups with 5 objects

A hungry crocodile wants a lot of food. Which set has more?

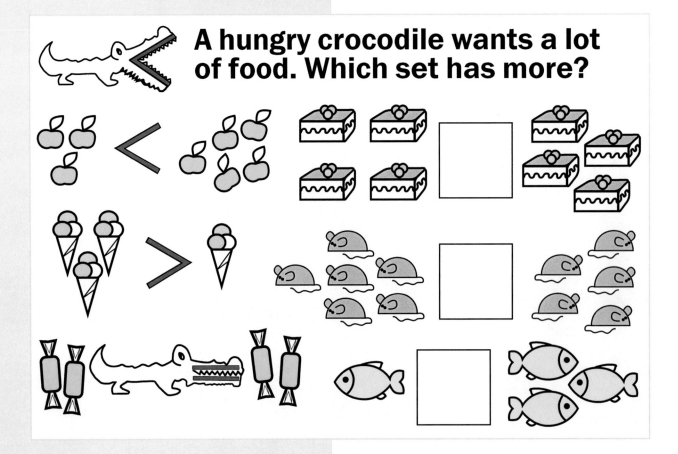

Write in the numbers on the train cars.
Color the trains with exactly 5 cars

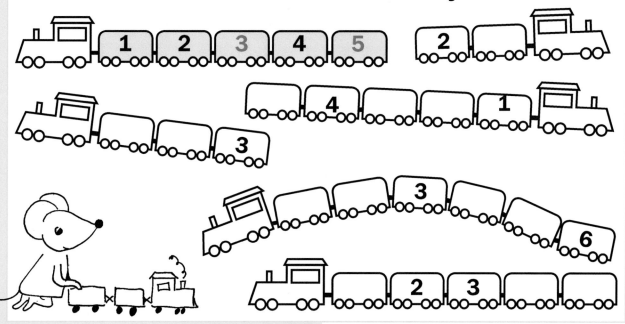

Draw in the missing pictures

Make trains with 5 cars

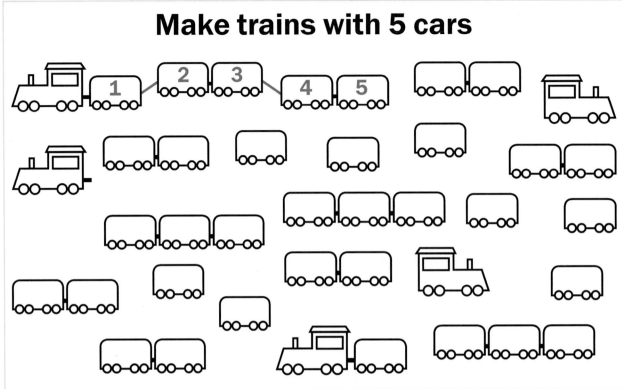

Match the same

COLORS   NUMBERS

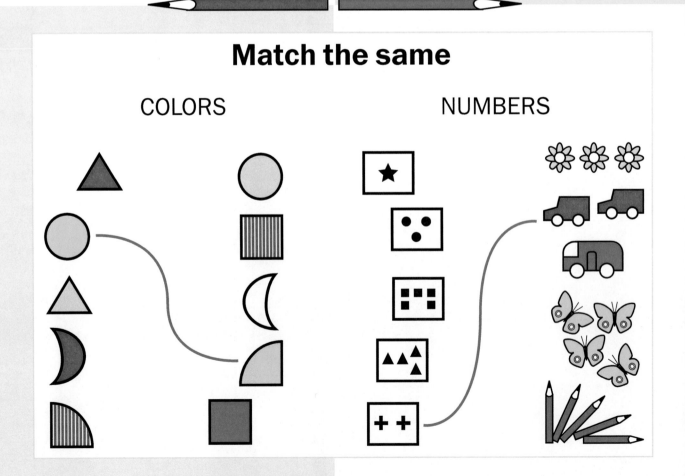

Fill the empty cells in the tables

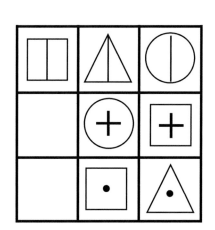

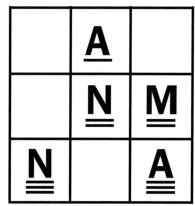

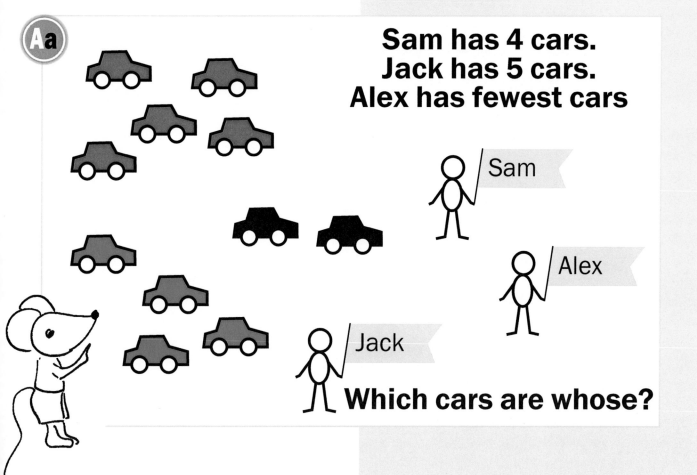

Sam has 4 cars.
Jack has 5 cars.
Alex has fewest cars

Sam

Alex

Jack

Which cars are whose?

Color the islands that have exactly 5 houses

Put in the arrows

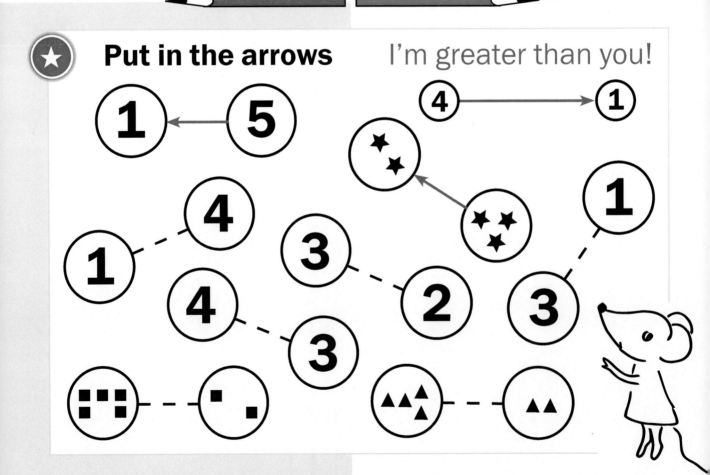

I'm greater than you!

Find the plates that have the same sets of candy

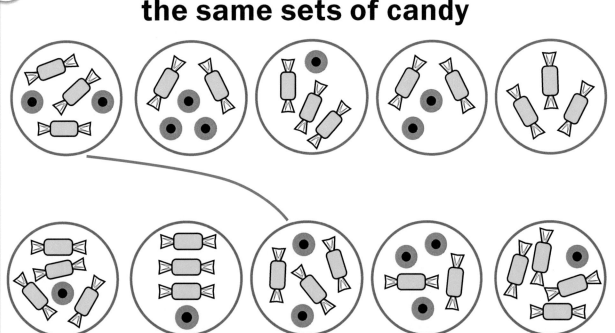

Write in the numbers on house floors. Color the floor that is higher than 3 but lower than 5

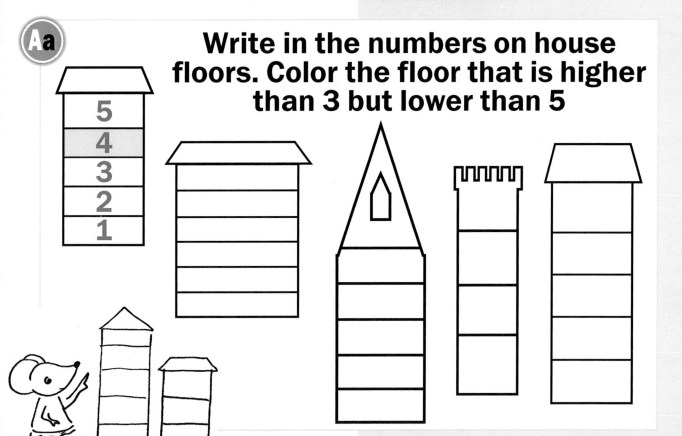

In each set, all pictures but one have the same shape. Circle the odd one out

Color brothers blue and sisters red

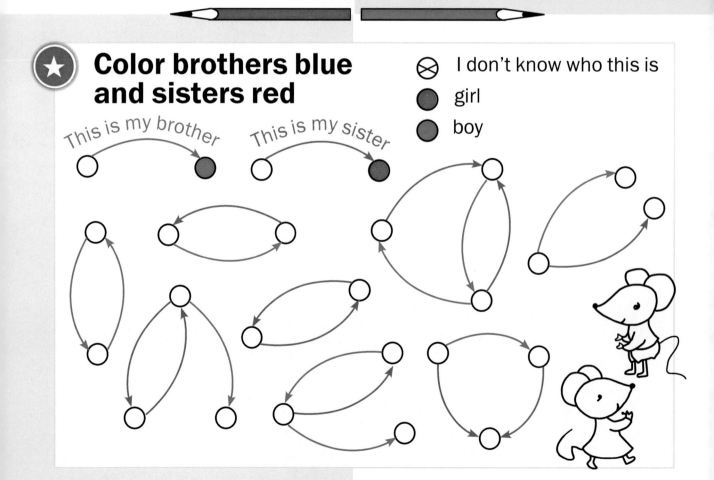

⊗ I don't know who this is

● girl

● boy

This is my brother

This is my sister

Circle the people who are heading toward the first car of the train

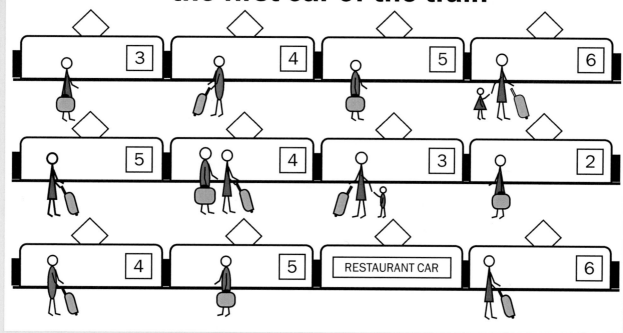

Use red to color the trucks carrying 4 crates
Use blue to color the trucks carrying 5 crates

3

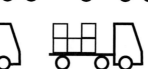

4

5

Help Jack and Jill split each chocolate into two equal parts

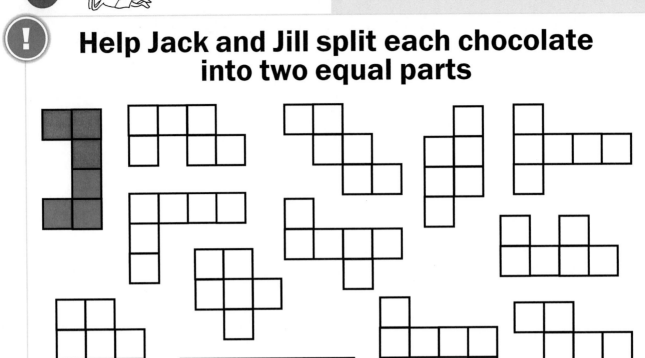

A hungry crocodile wants a lot of food. Which set has more?

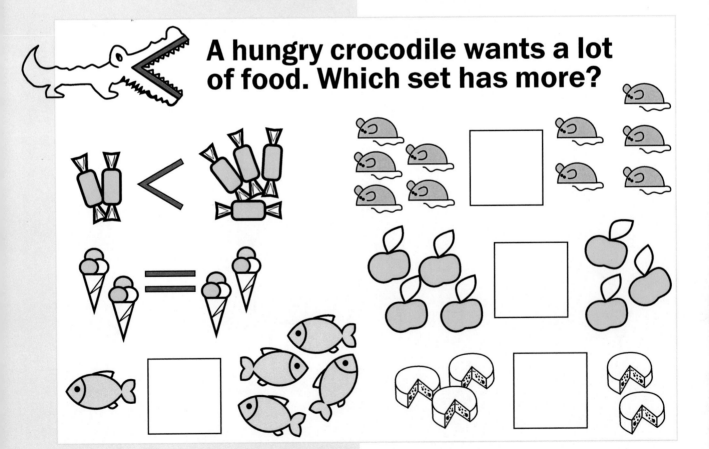

Connect the halves of the squares

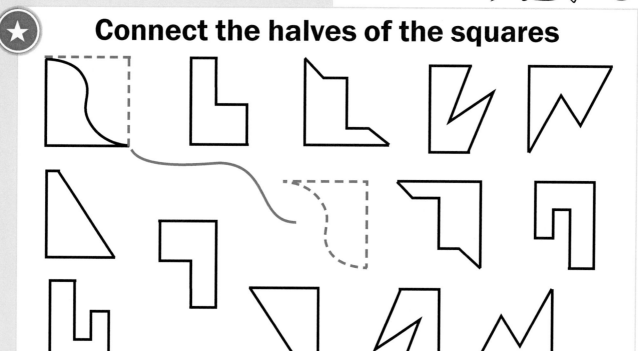

This is a picture Alex made: Circle the same pictures below

Draw in the shapes to balance the scales

Find this number snake: | 1 | 2 | 3 | 4 | 5 |

	5	4
5		3
2	1	2

5	4	5
2	3	
1	5	1

4	5	
3		4
2	1	2

5	2	
4	3	2
3		1

1	2	3
2		4
4	3	5

4	2	1
	3	
5	4	3

3	2	1
4		2
5	4	5

2	1	2
3		3
2	5	4

Use red to underline all the 5s.
Use blue to circle all the 4s.

1**4**5   24   41   57   65

52   34   214   123

543   105   72   15

38   504   94

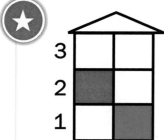

In each house,
use red to color the A2 square
Use blue to color the B1 square

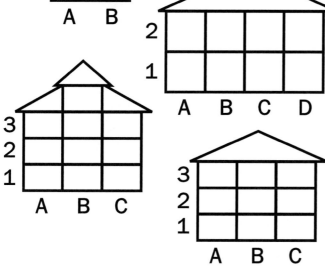

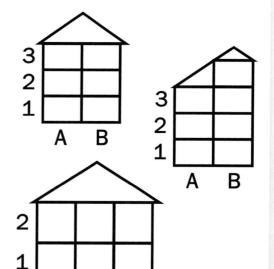

Fill the empty cells in the tables

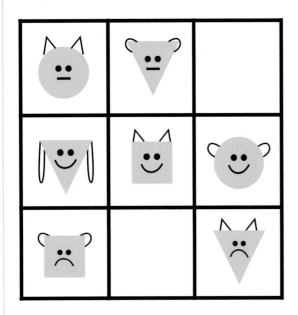
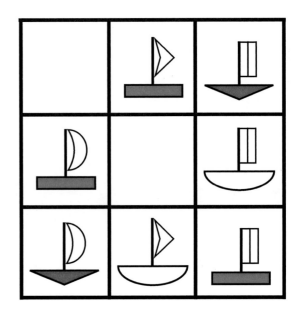

Connect the dots in counting order

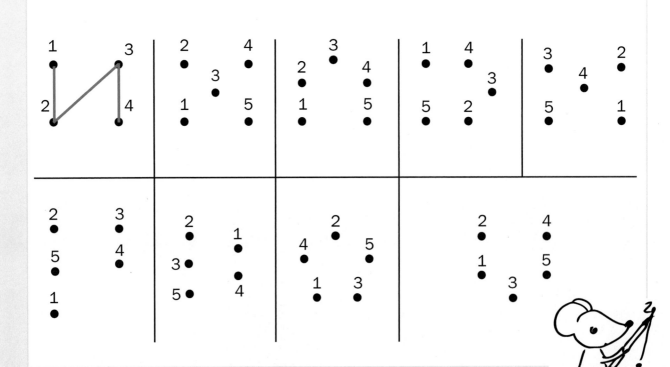

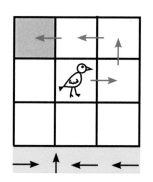 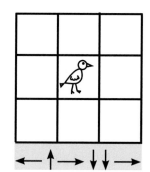

Where will the bird stop?

Color the end square.

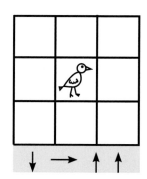 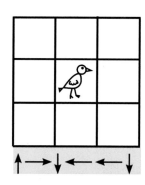 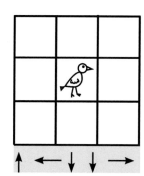 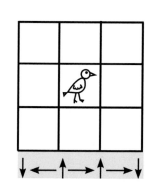

Continue the necklaces to match Mary's

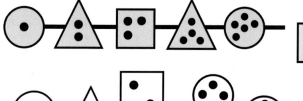
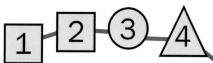

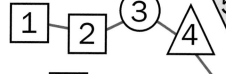

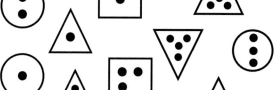

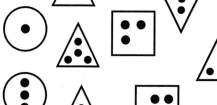

Cross out the squares with these coordinates

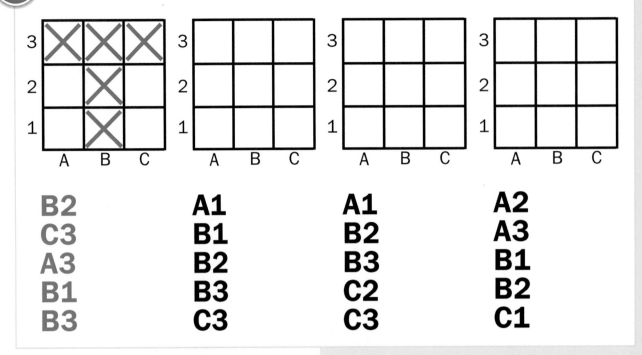

B2	A1	A1	A2
C3	B1	B2	A3
A3	B2	B3	B1
B1	B3	C2	B2
B3	C3	C3	C1

Which sticks did Mary move?
Color them

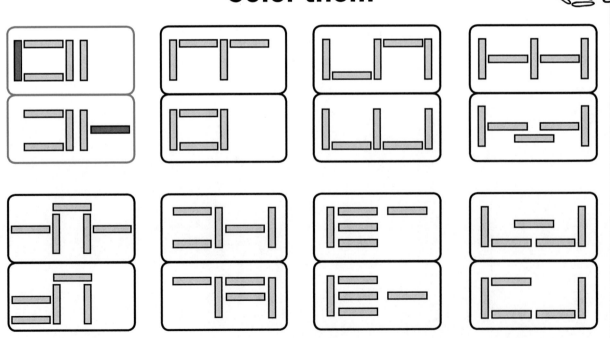

Divide into two figures that look like this:

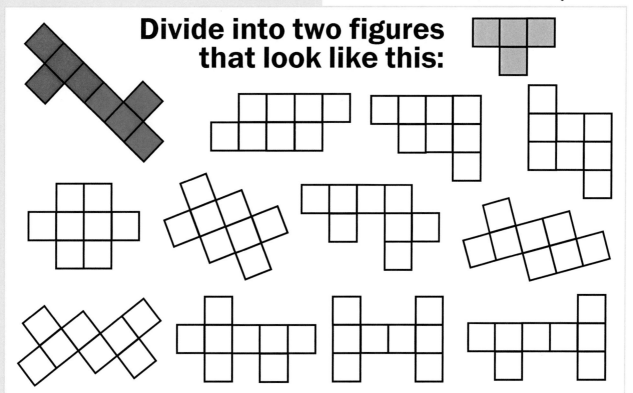

Draw a new path

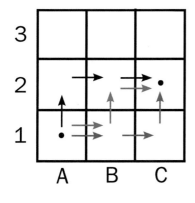

3
2
1

A B C

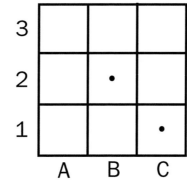

3
2
1

A B C

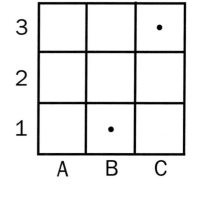

3
2
1

A B C

A1 ↑→→ **C2**
A1 →↑→ **C2**
A1 →→↑ **C2**

B2   **C1**
B2   **C1**
B2   **C1**

B1   **C3**
B1   **C3**
B1   **C3**

Connect the dots in order shown

3, 2, 4, 5, 1	5, 2, 1, 3, 4	5, 2, 4, 1, 3	1, 3, 2, 5, 4
1–2–3–1–4–5–1	1–2–3–1–4–2–5–1	1–2–3–4–5–1	1–2–3–1–4–5–1

1–2–3–4–5–3–1

1–2–5–4–3–2

Put in signs >, < or =

 >

  3   4

3   1

4   5

5   3

Jill has 5 red beads.
Jack has 5 blue beads.
How many are hidden?

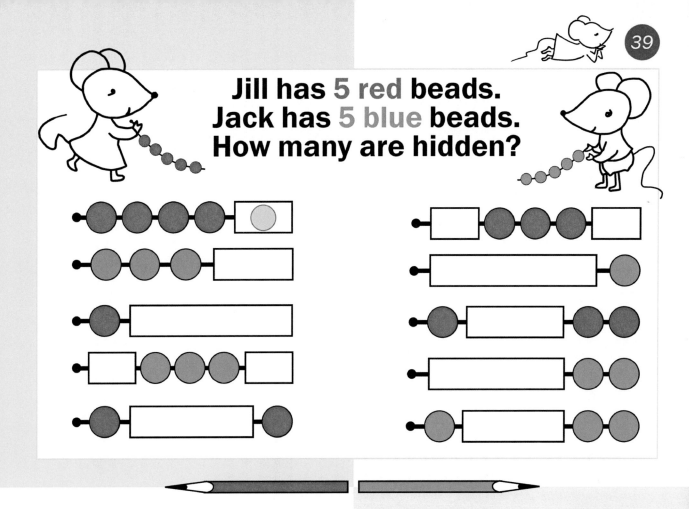

Divide into two figures
that look like this:

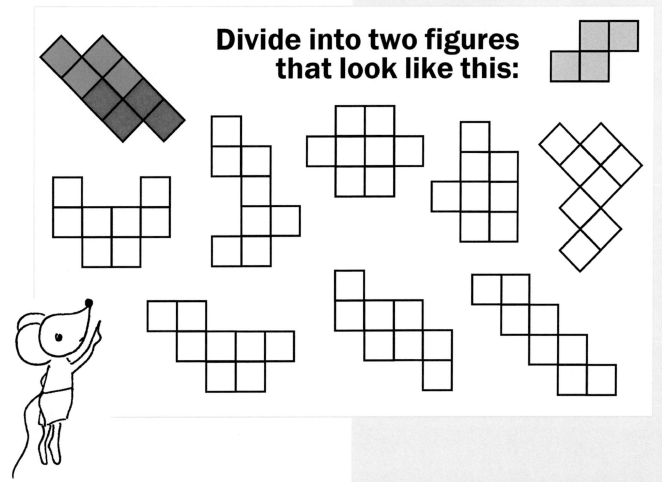

Go through the doors 1-2-3-4-5

3 | 5 | 3
| 3 | 3 |
1 | 3 | 4
| 2 | 4 |
2 | 2 | 5

2 | 2 | 5
| 2 | 4 |
1 | 3 | 4
| 3 | 5 |
4 | 4 | 3

| 2 | 2 |
1 | 3 | 3
| 3 | 4 |
2 | 1 | 5
| 2 | 5 |

Find a set of bricks for each house

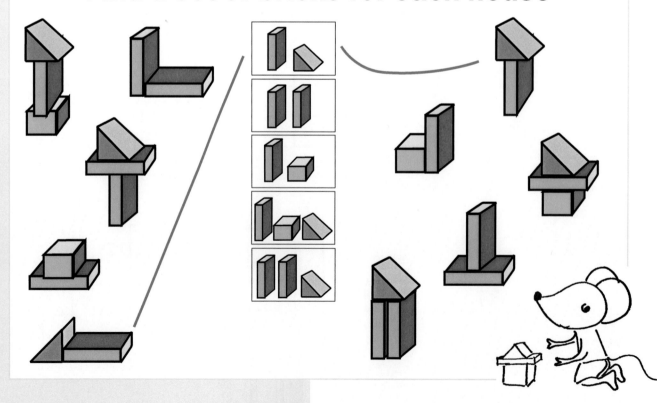

Aa Use red to circle words with 4 letters.
Use blue to circle words with 5 letters

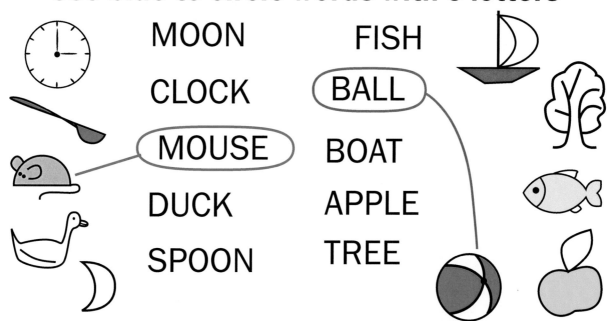

MOON   FISH

CLOCK   (BALL)

(MOUSE) BOAT

DUCK   APPLE

SPOON   TREE

★ Where will the bird stop?
Color the end square

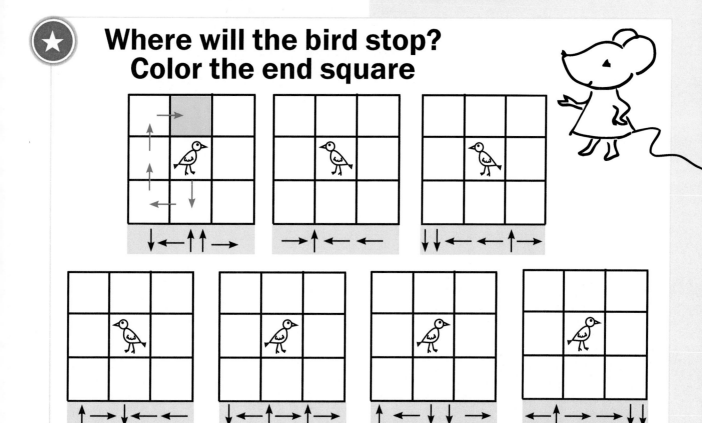

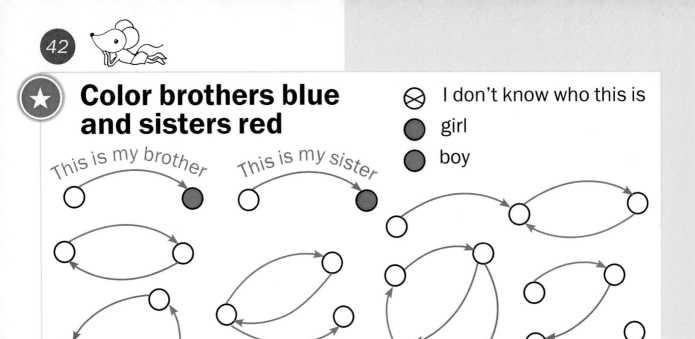

Color brothers blue and sisters red

⊗ I don't know who this is
● girl
● boy

This is my brother

This is my sister

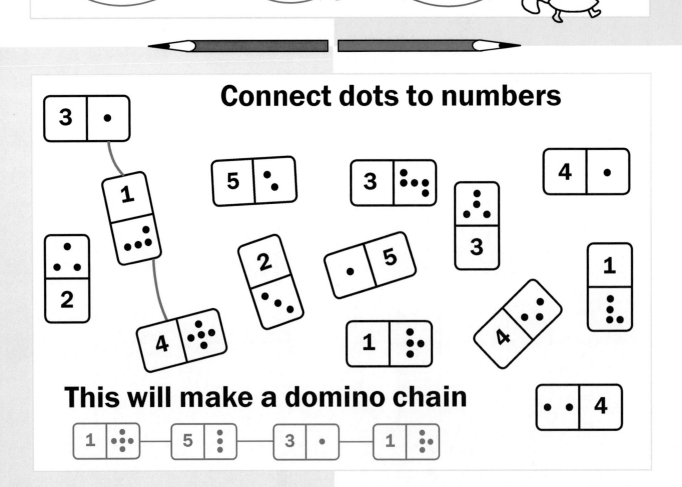

Connect dots to numbers

This will make a domino chain

How many cats are hiding?

___   ___

___   ___

Divide into two figures that look like this:

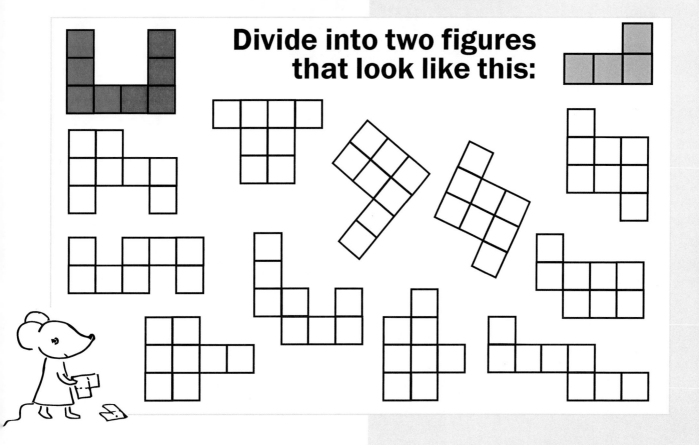

Connect from smallest to largest

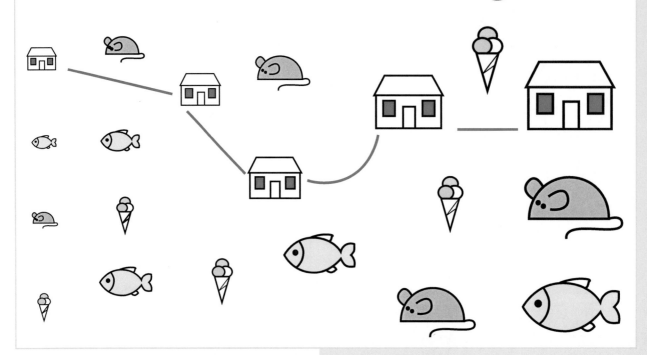

 Use **blue** to underline all the Os ,
Use **red** to underline all the As

FOOT	SALAD	WINDOW
OWL	HAT	CLOCK
SWAMP	PARROT	BOX
APPLE	CASTLE	BALL
BALLOT	FOOL	AIRPLANE

Circle the words with 2 of the same letter

Connect the dots in counting order

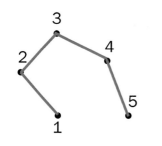

Help Jack and Jill split each chocolate into 2 equal parts

Cross out the squares with these coordinates

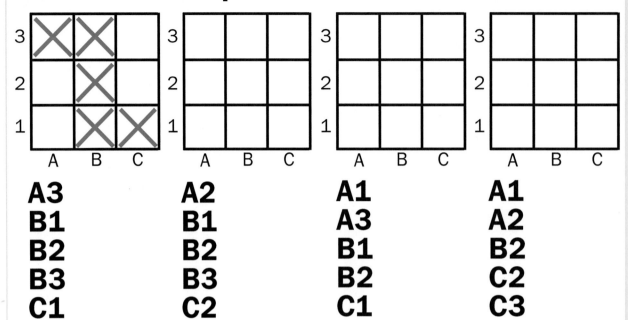

A3	A2	A1	A1
B1	B1	A3	A2
B2	B2	B1	B2
B3	B3	B2	C2
C1	C2	C1	C3

★ Write in the missing number
!

I'm greater than you!

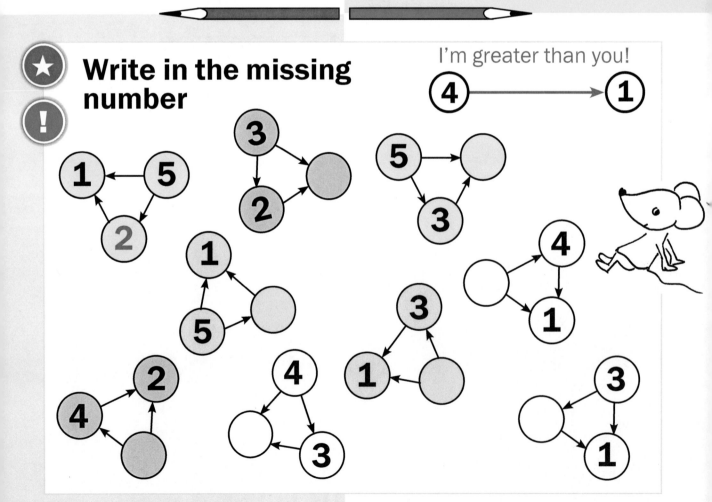

Find the towers made from the same sets of blocks. Color them the same

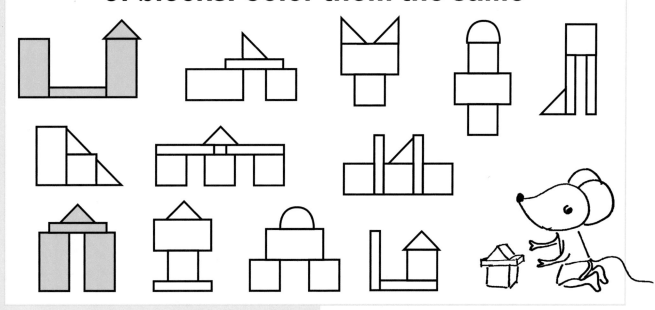

Use red to color the boats carrying 4 barrels.
Use blue to color the boats carrying 5 barrels

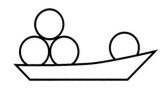

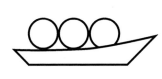
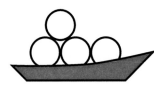
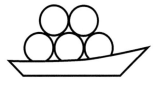

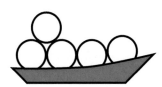
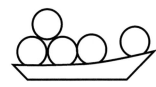
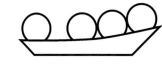

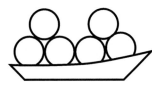

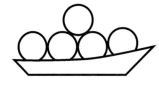

Find this number snake:

1	2	3	4	5

4	2	1
1	3	5
5	4	1

2	3	4
1	4	5
2	5	2

5	1	4
4	3	5
3	2	1

3	2	1
1	5	2
5	4	3

4	3	2
5	2	1
1	3	2

5	4	5
2	3	4
1	4	1

5	1	4
4	3	2
1	4	1

2	1	2
3	3	5
4	5	1

These apples were cut into halves.
Find sets that are the same

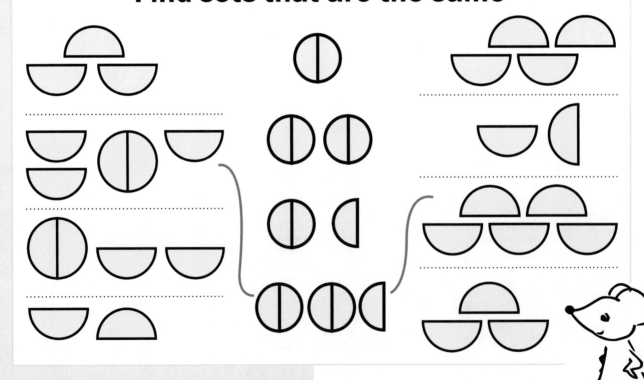

Help Jack and Jill split each chocolate into two equal parts

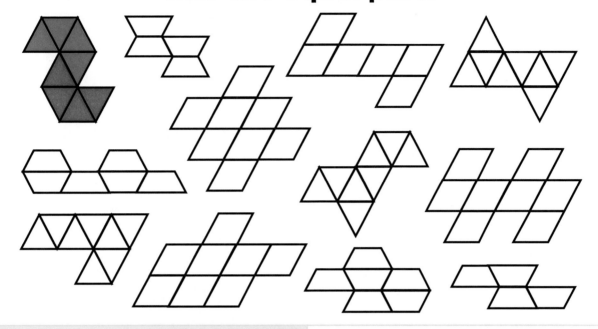

Fill the empty cells in the tables

Where is the set of bricks for each house?

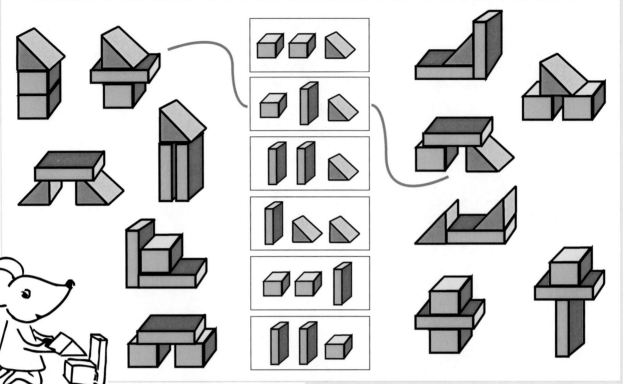

Draw balloons so that everybody has 5

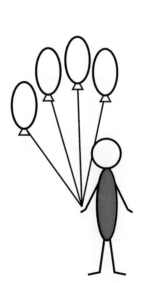

Cross out the squares with these coordinates

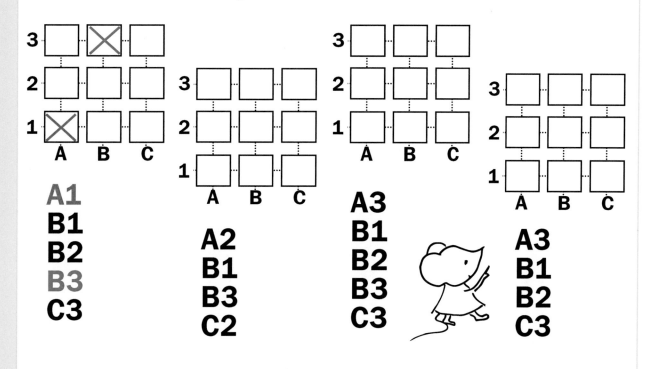

A1
B1
B2
B3
C3

A2
B1
B3
C2

A3
B1
B2
B3
C3

A3
B1
B2
C3

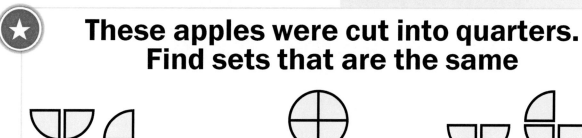

These apples were cut into quarters. Find sets that are the same

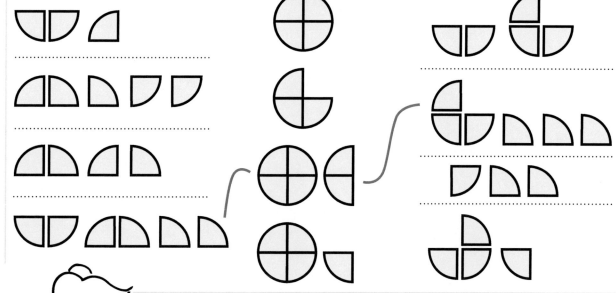

Replace the missing sticks

Find the identical butterflies

Use red to underline all the 5s.
Use blue to underline all the 4s.

5̲2   24   445   15   65

14̲5̲   520   43   240

74   504   410   49

914   74   567

Divide into figures that look like this:

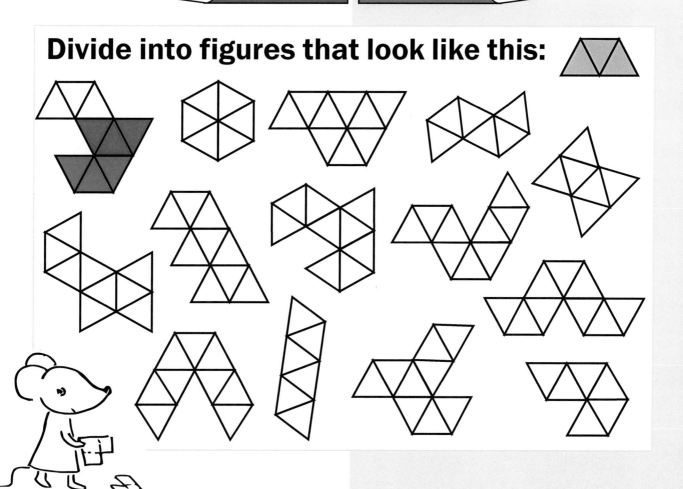

Color the stick that was moved to a different location

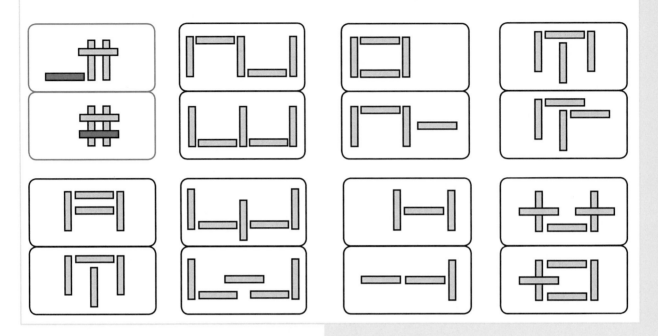

Collect sets of 3 pictures that are different in each feature

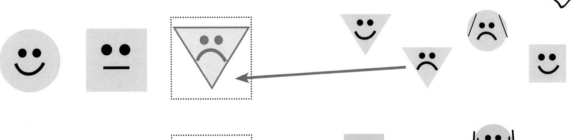

Complete the wings of the butterflies with dots and numbers

Help Jack and Jill split each chocolate into 2 equal parts

Cross out the squares with these coordinates

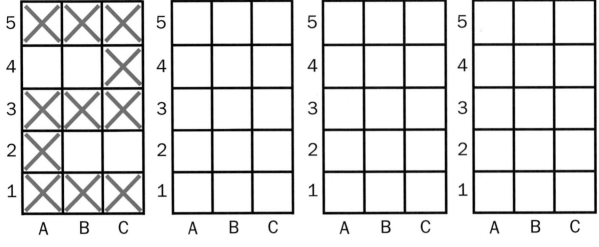

A1, A2, A3, A5, B1, C3, B5, C1, C3, C4, C5

A1, A3, A5, B1, Б3, B5, C1, C2, C3, C4, C5

A3, A4, A5, B3, C1, C2, C3, C4, C5

A1, A3, A4, A5, B1, C2, B3, B5, C1, C3, C5

There were 5 cherries on each branch. How many did Jack and Jill eat?

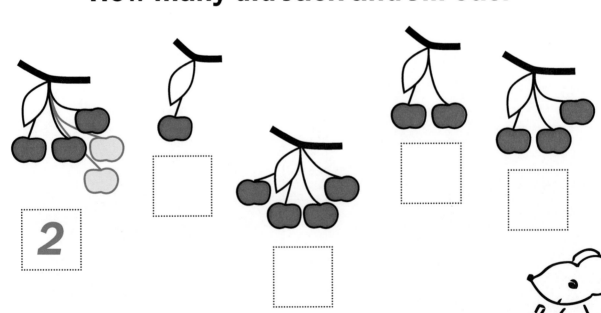

2

Circle the pictures made with exactly 5 sticks

Circle the houses made with these three building blocks:

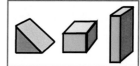

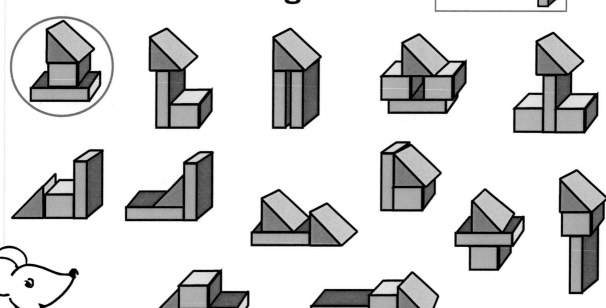

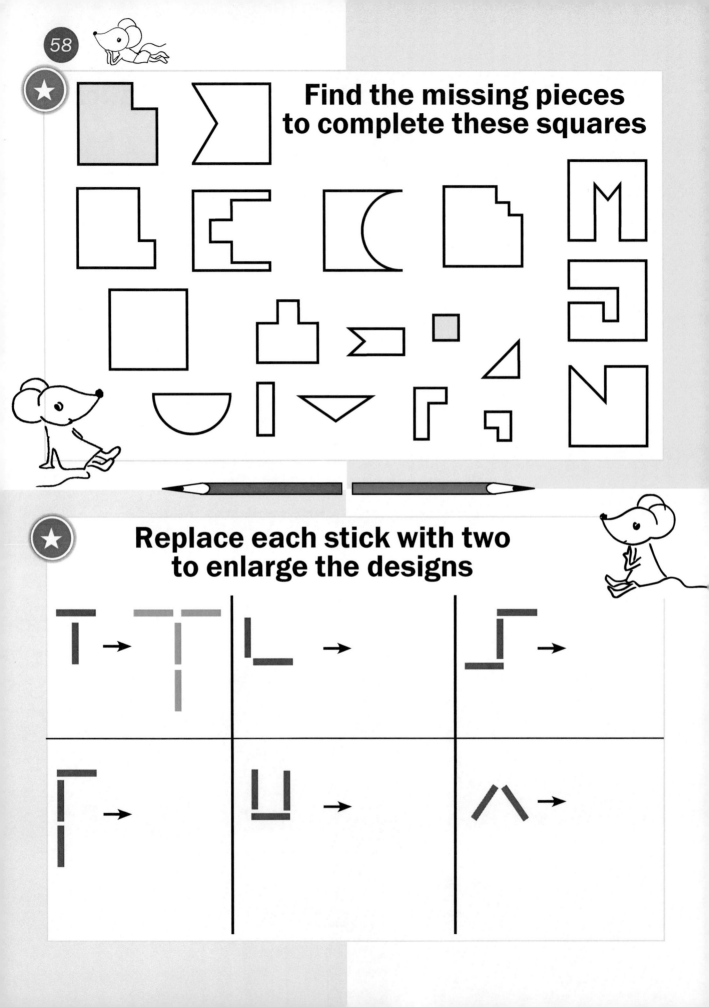

Find the missing pieces to complete these squares

Replace each stick with two to enlarge the designs

Find this number snake: | 1 | 2 | 3 | 4 | 5 |

4	1	2	3
2	3	2	4
5	3	2	5
4	1	4	2

	5		1
4	1	5	2
5	2	3	
4		4	5

2	4	5	
4	3	2	4
1	2		5
5		1	4

3	1		5
	2	4	2
2	3	2	
3	4	5	2

	3	4	
3		2	1
5	4	3	4
1	2		2

4		4	
3	2	1	2
4	2		3
5	3	4	

1	5	4	2
	4	3	
5	1	2	4
	5	3	

	5	2	
2	4	5	4
4	3	2	
2		1	5

Mary put her pictures down for a nap.
Draw the sleeping pictures

This is a picture John made: Circle the same pictures below

Mary is looking for her doll that looks like this: Circle the same doll below

Fill the empty cells in the tables

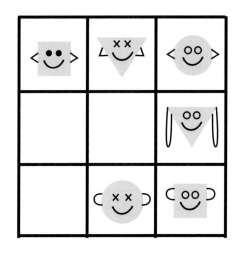 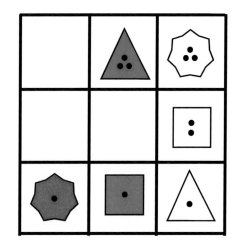

 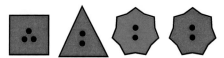

John has these pieces in his building set:

T T H H

Which towers could he have built?

Help Mary Mouse gather exactly five cherries in the maze

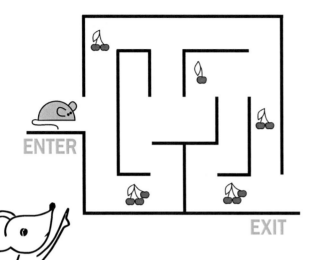

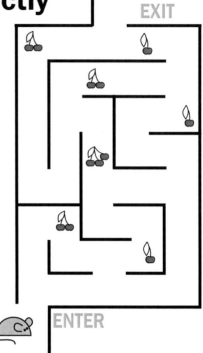

These are John's toys: Circle the same toys below

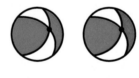 

In each set, all pictures but one have the same number of objects. Circle the odd one out

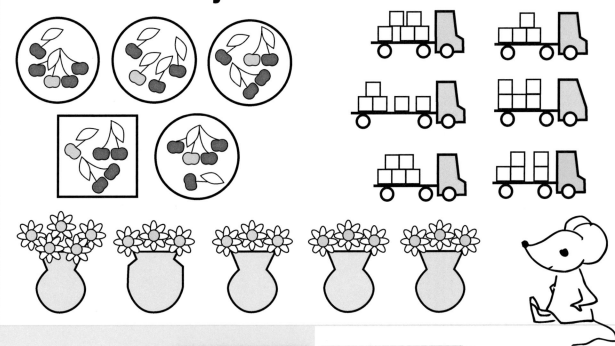

Make the pictures match

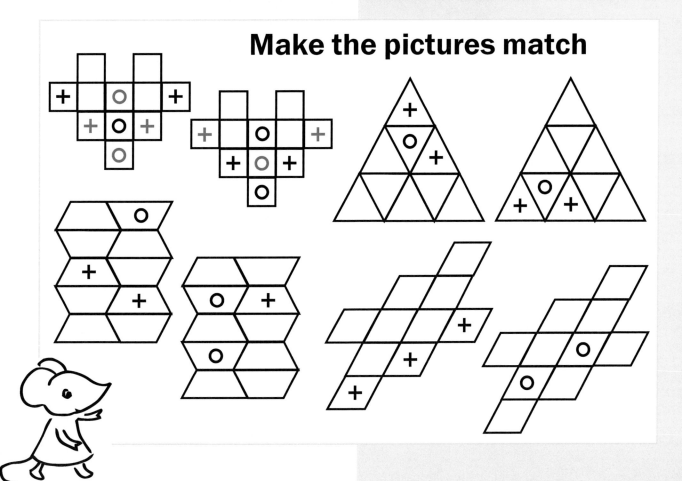

Jane Kats

MouseMatics

Learning Math the Fun Way

Workbook of Logic Problems for children ages 5-6

Translated by Lev and Sophia Roshal
Edited by Olga Lavut
Designed by Olga Lekhtonen

Made in the USA
San Bernardino, CA
09 December 2017